GOODNESS GRACIOUS!

An elephant goes from side to side.
He's very big and he's very wide.
And people say wherever he goes,
"Goodness gracious, what a nose!"

A turtle goes with a slippety-slop.
If she went much slower
she would stop.
And people say when they see her go
"Goodness gracious, aren't you slow!"

A pelican goes
with a swoop and a dive.
A school of fish has just arrived.
And people say
when he's had his fill,
"Goodness gracious, what a bill!"

A kangaroo goes with a jumpety-jump
His tail and legs go thumpety-thump.
And people say
when they watch him leap,
"Goodness gracious, what big feet!"

A tiger goes with a slink
and a glide.
Her patterned body helps her hide.
And people say
when they look at her,
"Goodness gracious, what sleek fur!"

A cheetah goes on four quiet feet.
The animals hide in case they meet.
And people say when he bounds past
"Goodness gracious, aren't you fast!"

Children go in lots of ways.
They run and jump,
as they laugh and play.
And people say to girls and boys...

"Goodness gracious, what a noise!"